# THE ART OF BWALING

– According to the Pink Dog –

*5 Simple Steps
to Release Life's
Messy Stress*

A lighthearted, inspirational gift book, filled with wit, canine wisdom, and a simple, practical approach to releasing stress.

By mounu and The Pink Dog

Copyright © 2016 all rights reserved. No part of this book may be reproduced in any form or by any electronic or mechanical means including storage and retrieval systems without permission in writing from Sharon mounu Riddell. Reviewers may quote brief passages in reviews. Disclaimer No part of this publication may be reproduced or transmitted in any form or by any means, mechanical or electronic, including photocopying or recording, or by any information storage and retrieval system, or transmitted by email without permission in writing from the publisher. While all attempts and efforts have been made to verify the information held within this publication, neither the author nor the publisher assumes any responsibility for errors, omissions, or opposing interpretations of the content herein. This book is for entertainment purposes only. The views expressed are those of the author alone, and should not be taken as expert instruction or commands. The reader of this book is responsible for his or her own actions when it comes to reading the book. Adherence to all applicable laws and regulations, including international, federal, state, and local governing professional licensing, business practices, advertising, and all other aspects of doing business in the US, Canada, or any other jurisdiction is the sole responsibility of the purchaser or reader. Neither the author nor the publisher assumes any responsibility or liability whatsoever on the behalf of the purchaser or reader of these materials. Any received slight of any individual or organization is purely unintentional.

Cover design & formatting by Perry Elisabeth Design | perryelisabethdesign.com

*This book is dedicated to Osho
for planting all these seeds.......
and to all the clients and friends
who have allowed me
to scatter these seeds
and watch them bloom.*

*I am so grateful
and
deeply blessed.*
-mounu

"Mounu has such a huge heart. She is a guide, and a comfort in times of great stress and fear, and a deeply generous spirit. In reading the first few lines of this book, I remembered to just BREATHE: the simplest thing, but so easy to forget. Thank you, Mounu, for always choosing Love, and reminding us of our own breath of life."
-Rosanne Cash

Singer-Songwriter-Author-Mother
Four-time Grammy award winner for her album The River and The thread
Author of "Composed"
http://www.rosannecash.com/


"In a day and age when it's hard not to take things too seriously, now is the time for a little mindful humor. Lap it up, laugh it up, and share these playful meditations with friends."
-Marilyn Schlitz, PhD

Author, researcher and Chair of PhD Psychology programs, Sofia University President Emeritus and Senior Fellow of The Institute of Noetic Sciences
Her most recent book is "Death Makes Life Possible".
http://marilynschlitz.com

"When I was competing in an LPGA tour event, Mounu wore a shirt that said "Breathe". Every time I saw her in the crowd, it reminded me to focus on my breath to control my anxiety of competition.
Mounu has helped me balance my life and my business. She has been my only consultant during all the highs and lows in life. She is my compass always pointing me to my true self."
-Nancy Quarcelino

LPGA Teaching & Club Professional "Hall of Fame Member".
Co-author of: "Staying on Course: Mastering Golf's Most Challenging Shots"
LPGA National Teacher of the Year 2000
Founder of Nancy Quarcelino School of Golf
http://www.qsog.com/


"We live in times that try our souls. If ever we needed to slow down, take a breath, let go and practice acceptance, surely it is now.
As mounu says in this wonderful little book, "Accepting the rains, the storms, the sun.." Easier said than done. Or is it? Maybe we've made acceptance out to be harder than it is. This book most certainly helps ease the path."
-Joe Calloway

Business Consultant Motivational Speaker
Author of seven books including
"Keep It Simple"
http://joecalloway.com/

"Imagine the possibilities when we embrace the simple yet transformational tools of 'is-ness' and 'bwaling'. Mounu breaks these tools into steps each of us can take. This book is lite, lively, and powerful."
-Jerry L. Campbell,

Psychotherapist
Nashville, TN


"Pink Dog and Mounu offer vital, simple, wise Truths to help us engage and embrace the beauty of Earthly experience. Open this book and you will be opened."
-Dawn Kirk,

Psychotherapist and Writer,
Nashville, TN
www.imaginetheshift.com

"Mounu has such a warm, big heart. What really strikes me about her, though, is the sense of consistency she has to offer. Grounded, kind and generous....When I read this book, it reminded me to take it easy and smile.

This little book is also a great reminder to breathe, if we just stop and breathe, the way will show itself to us."

-Paras Moghtader

Yoga student, teacher, Ayurvedic practitioner
Director of Moksha Yoga Brampton
http://brampton.mokshayoga.ca/


"Delightfully succinct wisdom on how to find ease and clarity during challenging times. Proof positive that deep truth lives in simplicity. Use this book to guide you through times of stress and find your own inner oasis."

-Adela Rubio,

Blogger and Virtual Event Host
http://adelarubio.com

*The Pink Dog is one of the wisest teachers I have ever had. She teaches by doing her 'being'. Moment by moment by moment she walks her talk. She breathes. She watches. She accepts and lets go instantly. (Unless of course she is chewing on her chew stick or her favorite toy.) She is always Here Now. She is always devoted, loyal and unconditionally loving, even after being reprimanded. She is an angel with four paws, my best friend and soul mate. She was either a human in her last go round or I was a dog. Whatever the case, I am very blessed and deeply grateful that God, Goddess, Great Spirit, Divinity or 'Watcha-ma-call-it' brought us together again.*
-Sharon mounu Riddell

Writer-Composer-Producer-Stress Management-Business and Spiritual Consultant

http://www.smounuriddell.com

http://www.angelsofafrica.org

Mounu and The Pink Dog would like to thank all the beautiful people who contributed their hearts, time and generous comments about our book.

We also want to thank our editorial support team. Elizabeth Trinkler and Mary Ruth Martin who patiently read and corrected every version of this little book as it evolved.

Also Solomon Shiv who graciously offered an in depth critique of the first version of the book which resulted in some changes that expanded and improved the current edition.

We love you all and we are humbled and grateful for your presence in our lives.

## Table of Contents

| | |
|---|---|
| Table of Contents | 11 |
| Introduction | 12 |
| Step 1: Breathe | 17 |
| Step 2: Watch | 23 |
| Step 3: Accept | 29 |
| Step 4: Let Go | 35 |
| Step 5: Practice – Practice – Practice | 41 |
| About the Authors | 47 |
| Coming soon! | 55 |

## Introduction

The recent events in our world have created a lot of toxic verbal and sometimes physical brawling.

For some, these events have created a lot of mental, emotional and gut wrenching bawling.

Now, more than ever, in order to recover and survive all the global challenges we face, not to mention our day to day 'life is messy and thus stressy' events, it's time to learn 'The Art of Bwaling. '

And how might you ask did I learn this fine art?

By living through life's messy stresses with the help of many friends and teachers, some of whom had fur, four paws and lots of unconditional love and devotion.

My first canine guru was my best friend and buddy 'Taffy' and my most recent teachers have been Joshy, Emmy and Cakes.

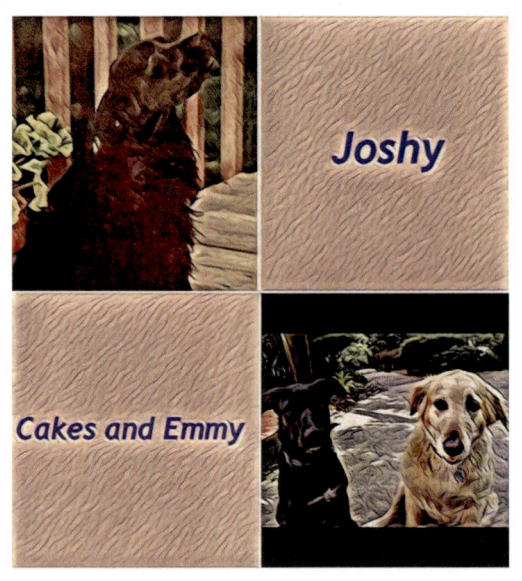

*Joshy*

*Cakes and Emmy*

My current teacher, guru and Sensei is The Pink Dog. She shows me, every moment of everyday, how to live this book. And she does it so effortlessly.

As for me, I have to practice, practice, practice and remember to have a Bwal while I'm at it!

So The Pink Dog and I want to welcome you to the Bwal and the delightful Art of Bwaling.

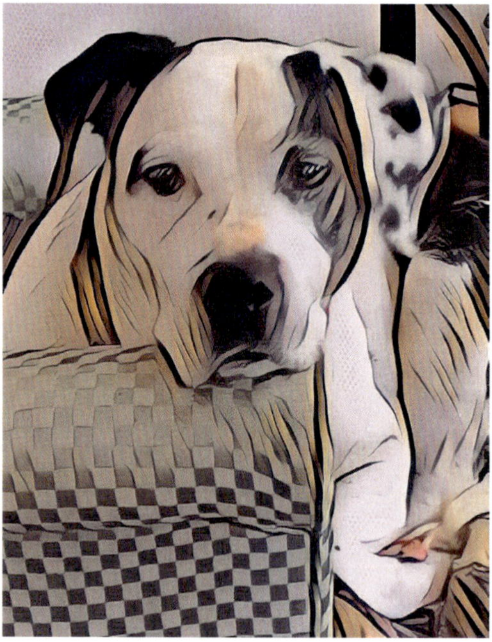

## Step 1
## Breathe

Moment by moment we get to choose
The act of reacting is how we loose

Ourself-Our wits-Our love-Our peace
But response-ability's within our reach

A single breath and we can breach
That sea of anger-fear-dispair
Pulling us down to who knows where

Did I really say that
What did I do
Lost myself - Offended you
All because I forgot to breathe

Reaction thus delayed reprieve
Here comes my pain – my wounds - my fright
Assaulting everything in sight

Lashing out
I'm quite insane
Replaying old worn-out refrains

I've got to win-I've got to fight
Too late to catch that save me flight

If only I could catch my breath
I might escape what feels like death

Or better yet just simply breathe
Ah Yes! There is that sweet reprieve

I had that choice ability
Right from the start inside of me
Respond-react-go up-go down
Choose or lose-swim or drown

Moment by moment we can receive
The gift of life if we'll just breathe

# BREATHE

## Step 2
## Watch

Now if we are to attend the Bwal
Instead of the bawl - worse yet - the brawl

We have to watch with eagle's eye
The patient heart of the butterfly

The ferocious soul that must be free
From monkey mind's captivity

We have to watch then watch some more
If we are to find the door

That isn't locked - or closed - or there
AH - there's the rub - the joke - the snare
We seek a door that isn't there

Yet we're confined - we are not free
We ask ourselves how can this be

We're elephants quite large and strong
With just a chain - no lock - what's wrong

We've all been trained - we're in a cage
It's way past time to turn the page

Step into truth that sets us free
We need to watch-we need to see
Illusion's grim reality

Observe! Observe! And it will change
Observer too is rearranged


For in the act of watching we
Will be set free eventually

# WATCH

# Step 3
# Accept

Except if we do not accept
We never will become adept
At letting isness simply be
Whatever it is momentarily

Oh no not that - I can't abide
What's happening so I must hide
Or run - or scream - or have a fit
What's happening now just can't be it

It simply cannot be this way
I must deny - I won't obey
What's staring me right in the face
Is utter - total - sheer disgrace
And thus it cannot possibly
Be a fact - I disagree
I won't accept - I will deny
Resist until I cry or die

Yet isness is - and ain'tness ain't
When I accept I'll be a saint

Saint Redemption at long last
Got no future - got no past

Only now - that's all we need
Acceptance is our freedom seed

Moment by moment we plant - we till
Then blossom like the daffodil
Accepting the rain, the storms, the sun
We learn that life can be quite fun

This! Only this in the sweet here now
All we can say is wow! Holy cow

# ACCEPT

## STEP 4
## LET GO

Alas! The Bwal is not complete
One more dance! Get on your feet

For this is the hardest dance of all
At the 'Get yourself free and have a Bwal Ball'

Or the easiest as the case may be
It all depends on you and me

If we become like falling leaves
Rather than the one that cleaves
Letting go will be a cinch
Instead of that total body clinch

For most of us the fear of loss
Turns us into ancient moss
Clinging to what's dead and gone
Way too tightly-way too long

I must hold on or I will die
While life is swiftly passing by
And I'm not even on the train
Stuck at the station of stress and strain

But I have to hold this pain at bay
Or surely I will rue the day
I can't let go-I'll disappear
Or drown inside unyielding tears

'Just let it go' says all the they
'But just exactly how' I say

First take a breath-then watch and see

Acceptance then will set you free

Just like those leaves
We too can fall

And have ourselves a freedom Bwal

# LET GO

## STEP 5
## PRACTICE – PRACTICE – PRACTICE

One final step

Now it's all up to you
And Yes my dear Bwaler
All Your Dreams can come true

For now that you've learned this
    lost, simple art
All you need to do now is begin

    So just start

Take a step then another
And then just one more
Soon you will find yourself out on the floor
Spinning away all your troubles and cares
Waltzing away from all of life's snares

The messy, the stressy
The brawls and the bawls
Jitterbugging your way
To wherever heart calls

Just breathing and watching
Accepting it all
Then letting it go
That's the dance
That's the Bwal

And now that you've learned
    this new ancient art
You must practice and practice and practice
    your part
You just have to be willing
It doesn't take smarts

All it takes is attention

    And all of your heart

So why are you waiting
Jump
    Leap
        Dive

# S<small>TART</small>

# Practice Practice Practice

## About the Authors:

## The Pink Dog

The Pink Dog was rescued, literally, from a rugged life on the streets. She appeared one day at an office door, in downtown Music City. Erik, the son of the business owner, Elizabeth Trinkler, was her knight in shining armor, when he looked plaintively at his Mom with eyes that begged, 'Can we keep her?'

She spent some wild and wooly years with Liz at Birdsong Lodge in Ashland City, where she refined her escape artist skills in pursuit of the neighbors chickens.

She found her way to her co-writer, when she and Liz moved into town to share a house with mounu.

She and mounu quickly recognized their bond of many lifetimes. It was through this relationship that The Pink Dog remembered her lifetime as the Sentry for The Tavern of The Divine. Sharing her many stories about this time has resulted in The Pink Dog Chronicles from The Tavern of The Divine.

This book is the Prequel to that 'coming soon' series.

Erik, The Pink Dog's Knight in shining armor, with his daughter Della.

Liz and The Pink Dog.

Sharon mounu Riddell is a writer, composer and producer who lives in Nashville, TN. She is also a Stress Management, Business and Spiritual consultant.

She has spent most of her life actively involved in creating music, inspirational writing and exploring visionary solutions for the challenges facing our world.

After retiring from full time performing on the road, she has focused on consulting, writing and producing for humanitarian projects.

One of her songs 'Let Love Ring' written on 9/11 was the catalyst for a day long remembrance on the first anniversary of that event. The Tennessee legislature declared 9.11.2002 'Let Love Ring Day'. She is the founder of The Angels of Africa Project.

The centerpiece of the project is a musical play consisting of twelve songs and twelve character stories, each depicting a different aspect of the orphan pandemic in Sub-Saharan Africa. The play was written for two-time Tony nominee Ernestine Jackson.

She is the founder of the 'Love Dreams for The Planet Project'. The project is developing a music video of Ms. Jackson singing two of mounu's songs. Mounu believes that music can heal, uplift and inspire change.

**LOVE DREAMS FOR THE PLANET PROJECT**

She believes that Love Is The Power and The Way, the title of one of the songs in the video.

The project will create a community of dreamers and storytellers who will write a new American Dream. The vision of the project is to donate the video to schools and churches in order to allow our children, the most creative among us, to share their stories and dreams.

In addition to all her other projects, mounu and The Pink Dog are currently at work on The Pink Dog Chronicles from The Tavern of The Divine.

A series that will continue to share the lighthearted, stress releasing, spiritual canine wisdom that produced The Art of Bwaling......According to The Pink Dog.

While this may look like
~~The End~~
It is really just
~~The Beginning~~

Really!

## Coming soon!

The Pink Dog Chronicles from The Tavern of The Divine. In this series the pink dog will be inviting all of her readers to dive deep inside themselves and discover The Tavern of The Divine.

Sipping and soaring and singing is all there is to do in the tavern. This comes naturally after sipping on the Tavern's wine. The Tavern offers four vintage selections: Divine Love ~ Boundless Bliss ~ Rapturous Joy - Infinite Peace.

In this series The Pink Dog will be sharing her stress releasing wisdom on a variety of topics including: Aging ~ Gratitude ~ Grace ~ Gestation ~ Problems ~ Quantum Physics ~ Infinity and many other lighthearted issues, in her own humorous, Seussian way.

She offers you a little sample to whet your appetite for deep diving into The Tavern of The Divine.

So I said, 'Jesus - Is that you?'
Could this be real - Could this be true
Then through the mist - the haze - the fog
Those eyes belonged to The Pink Dog
The Sentry at The Tavern's door
Where lost souls come to sip and soar
And learn The Tavern's just the place
To leave behind that ole rat race
While sipping on that Joy divine
The Tavern's ancient, vintage wine
That soothes those weary, dreary blues
Of those who've overpaid their dues
And lost their soul's heart dancing shoes

Excerpt from the first edition of The Pink Dog Chronicles. 2016

Contact mounu and The Pink Dog at:
www.smounuriddell.com
mounumi@comcast.net

Follow them on Face Book: @Sharon mounu Riddell
And: Love Dreams for The Planet Project

Instagram: @mounumi

Twitter: @mounumi

S. mounu Riddell and The Pink Dog
11.10.2015
SmR Productions
2016

Made in the USA
Middletown, DE
16 October 2017